SIX SUITES for VIOLA

(originally for Cello)

by

J. S. BACH

Transcribed by Watson Forbes

PREFACE

Text. Bach's autograph manuscript of these Cello Suites has never been found. For this edition, the editor has consulted principally the authoritative Bach-Gesellschaft edition together with a facsimile of the manuscript copied by Bach's second wife, Anna Magdalena.

The viola part, in the first five suites, appears one octave higher than in the original for cello. Suite No. 6 was composed for a five stringed instrument tuned thus :—

Since Bach makes full use of all five strings, only a five stringed instrument can really do justice to the music. Transposition to an octave higher presents the viola player with many awkward fingerings, renders many chords impracticable and also makes frequent use of the upper register of the viola—thus introducing a tone colour which is not very suitable for this type of music. For practical reasons, the suite has therefore been transposed from the original key of D major to G major. This transcription has been freely adapted to keep the viola part within a compass similar to that employed in the previous suites. It has also been found possible to reproduce, in this key, most of the chords as they appear in the original.

Tempo. Bach left no indication of tempo for any of the movements ; suggestions for tempo, including metronome marks, have been added by the editor.

Marks of Expression. There are no marks of expression in the original except for some rather obvious " echo " effects (cf. Prelude to Suite No. 6). Those indicated by the editor are suggestions only and may be altered or elaborated at the player's discretion.

Bowing. The Anna Magdalena manuscript has bowing marks—presumably taken from Bach's autograph score. These bowings are an essential part of this music and, though they are sometimes a little vague in the Anna Magdalena copy—and occasionally even omitted—the bowings in this present edition are based largely on this manuscript ; the bowings in the Bach-Gesellschaft edition have also been taken into consideration.

In order to keep the text clear, the style of bowing is shown only in the first few bars of each movement. Where necessary, this is further commented upon in footnotes. Unless otherwise marked, the player should apply the same style of bowing throughout the movement.

" Upper half of bow "—from middle to point.

" Lower half of bow "—from heel to middle.

Chords. Held chords should be broken in the normal way. In quick tempo, all the notes of a chord should be played together if possible, while in accompanied melody, only the melody note should be sustained. Suggestions as to the best method of performance are included in the text as footnotes.

Performance. Whenever possible, all the repeats should be played ; in some of the longer movements, however, it is often more expedient to treat them as optional. The timing of each suite is based on performances where all repeats have been made.

W.F.

SUITE № 1

Time of performance 15 mins.

J. S. BACH

Transcribed by WATSON FORBES

WARNING: The unauthorised copying of the whole or any part of this publication is illegal and can lead to prosecution.

poco a poco a tempo

rit.   *f*   *p*   cresc.

mf   cresc.

f

p

Sul D

Sul A—

p   cresc.

f

allargando

$2\frac{1}{2}$ mins.

Allemande Moderato ♩ = 80

*Alternative bowing shown above and below the notes

Courante Allegro ♩ = 120

*f *marcato*

p *cresc.*

f

f

mf

p sub. cresc.

f

2 mins.

*On the string, upper half of bow (quasi martellato.)

Sarabande Lento ♪ = 80*

p espressivo

poco f

p

$2\frac{1}{2}$ mins.

Menuetto I Moderato ♩ = 120

mf

mf

cresc.

f

Fine.

3 mins.

*Think of the music in three slow crotchet beats.

† Phrase the second note of each slur

†† Heavy spiccato; lower half of bow.

Menuetto II

Menuetto I D.C.

Gigue Allegro vivace ♩. = 116

* Gentle detached strokes, on the string; upper half of bow.

† Lower half of bow.

1¼ mins.

SUITE № 2

Time of performance 17 mins.

J. S. BACH
Transcribed by WATSON FORBES

Prélude Andante ♩ = 58-72

cresc. e più animato (♩ = 72)

a tempo

p tranquillo (♩ = 58)

3¼ mins.

Allemande Moderato ♩ = 72

* Alternative bowing shown above and below the notes.

3 mins.

Courante Allegro ♩ = 120

*A light detaché; upper half of bow.

1½ mins.

Sarabande Lento ♪ = 80*

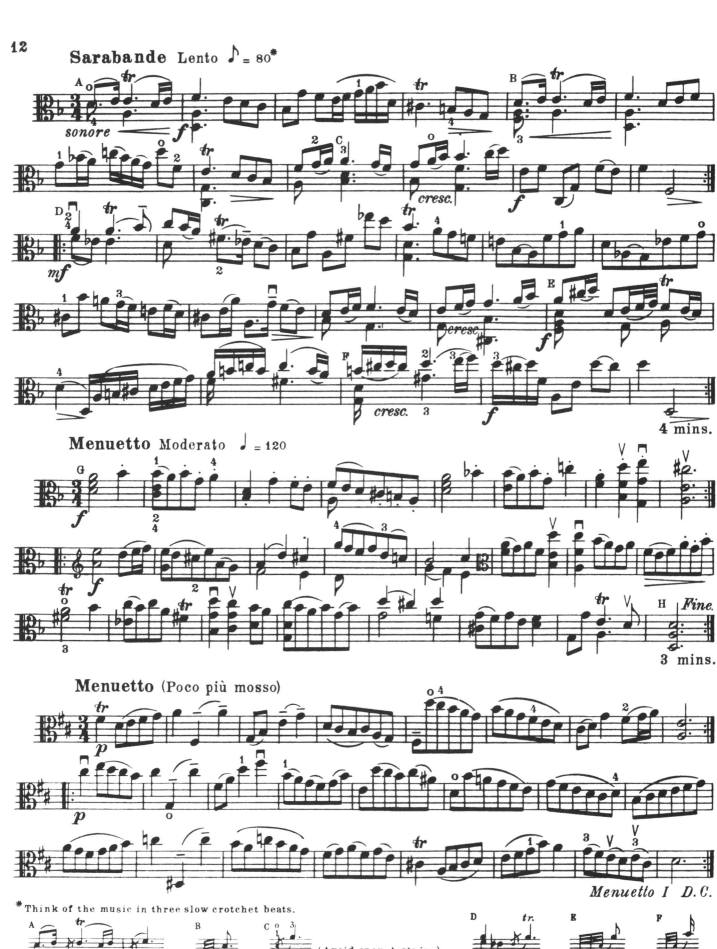

4 mins.

Menuetto Moderato ♩ = 120

Fine.

3 mins.

Menuetto (Poco più mosso)

Menuetto I *D.C.*

*Think of the music in three slow crotchet beats.

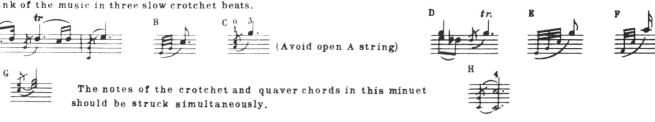

(Avoid open A string)

The notes of the crotchet and quaver chords in this minuet
should be struck simultaneously.

Gigue Vivace ♩.= 76

*f marcato**

f

mf

sfz

f

cresc.

sfz f

2 mins.

＊ Between the heel and middle of bow.

† Alternative bowing shown above and below the notes.

SUITE Nº 3

Time of performance 18 mins.

J. S. BACH

Transcribed by WATSON FORBES

Prélude Allegro moderato ♩ = 92

* From here onwards, alternative bowings are shown above and below the notes.

3 mins.

Allemande Moderato ♩ = 72

* Long spiccato at the heel.

† Heel, short spiccato.

3 mins.

Courante Allegro ♩. = 69

* Long detaché; upper half of bow.

2½ mins.

Sarabande Lento ♪ = 100

3 mins.

Bourrée I Allegretto ♩ = 84

poco f grazioso

* Spiccato, but not too short; towards the heel of the bow.

Bourrée II Poco meno mosso ♩= 76

Bourrée I D.C.

† Longer stokes, more tenuto, but not legato; above the middle of the bow.

Gigue Vivace ♩. = 80

*A vigorous stroke towards the heel of the bow.   † Middle of the bow.

†† Heavy staccato at the heel.

3 mins.

SUITE Nº 4

Time of performance 20 mins.

J. S. BACH
Transcribed by WATSON FORBES

Prélude Maestoso ♩ = 72

poco allarg.

*A legato stroke in the upper half of the bow; well "into the string."

Allemande Moderato ♩ = 76

p legato

poco cresc.

mf   dim.

p

cresc.

mp

cresc.   mf

(♭)   (♭)   (♮)

D—
p

cresc.   mf   dim.

p

cresc.   mf

A   B

* Phrase in quaver beats.

4 ½ mins.

Courante Allegro ♩ = 152

* **Middle of the bow, slightly lifted.**

† **Alternative bowing shown above and below the notes.**

2½ mins.

26

Sarabande Lento ♩ = 100

4 mins.

Bourrée I Allegretto ♩ = 92

or sustain all three notes if possible.

*Upper half, poco staccato but not martellato

Bourrée II

Fine.

4 mins.

† Lower half of bow.

Bourrée I D.C.

28

Gigue Allegro vivace ♩. = 160

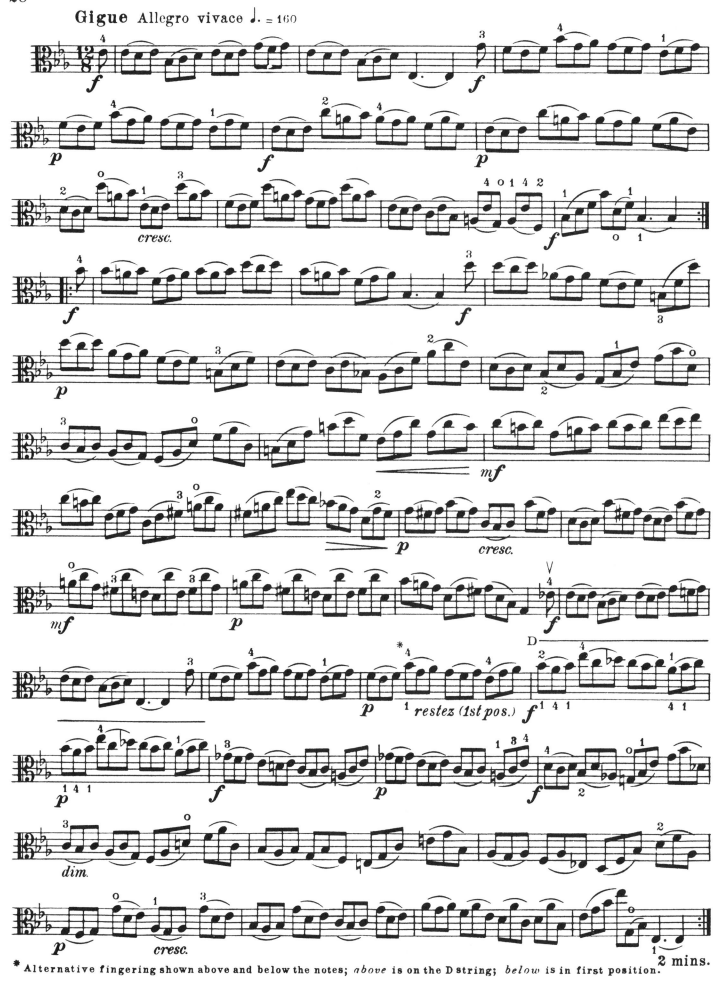

* Alternative fingering shown above and below the notes; *above* is on the D string; *below* is in first position.

2 mins.

SUITE № 5*

Time of performance 22 mins.

J. S. BACH

Transcribed by WATSON FORBES

Prélude Adagio ♪ = 88

*In the original, Bach wrote for a Cello with the A string tuned down to G. This transcription for Viola reverts to the normal tuning (The notes of a few chords have had to be redistributed.)

Thus:-

Allegro ♩. = 72

* A light stroke, on the string; upper half of bow.

5½ mins.

Courante Allegro ma non troppo ♩= 72

Sarabande Lento ♪ = 76

2 mins.

3¼ mins.

*This is the French form of Courante, all the others in these suites being of the Italian type (coranto.) Mark well the typical ⁶⁄₄ rhythm in the cadence bars.

† Really in three very slow beats; rather free (rubato) and meditative in style.

Gavotte I Allegretto ♩ = 80

Gavotte II Poco più mosso ♩ = 88

Gavotte I D.C.

A The three notes of the chords to be struck together; heel of bow.

Gigue Allegretto ♩. = 69

2 mins.

SUITE № 6*

Time of performance 27 mins.

J. S. BACH

Transcribed by WATSON FORBES

Prélude Allegro moderato ♩. = 92

* See note on this suite in the preface

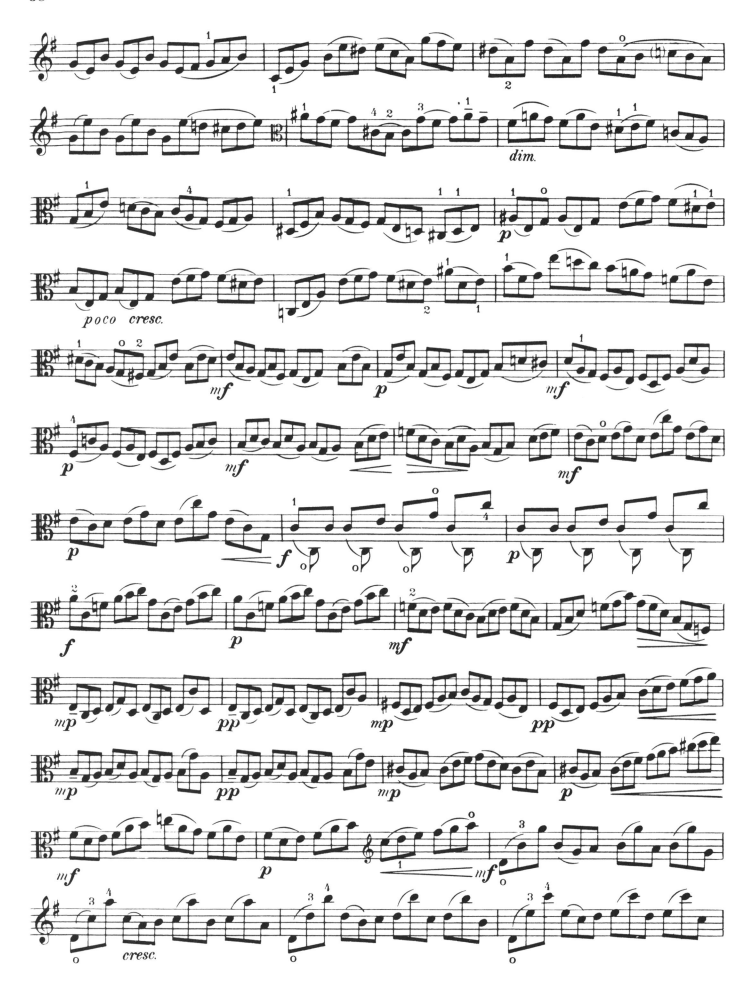

4½ mins.

Allemande Moderato ♪ = 60*

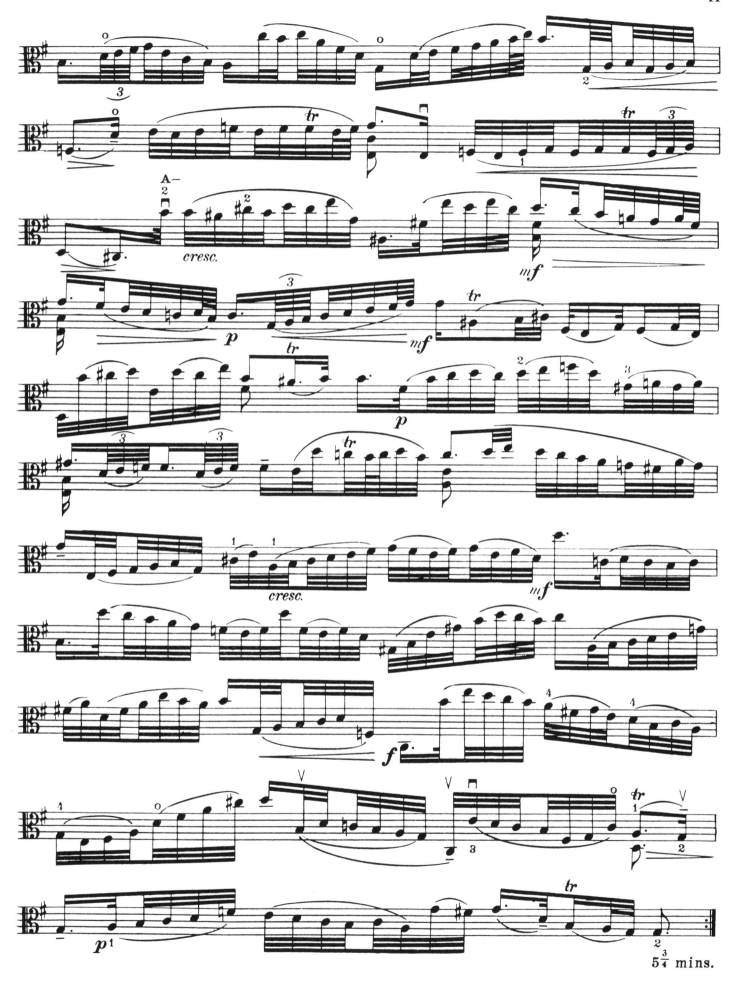

$5\frac{3}{4}$ mins.

Courante Allegro ♩ = 152

mf (on the string)

p leggiero

cresc.

mf

cresc.

f

mf

* Upper half of the bow; poco martellato

3 mins.

Sarabande Lento ♩ = 54

f sostenuto

meno *f*

cresc.

4½ mins.

A
Sustain the two upper
parts wherever possible:-

A The notes of the chords to be played together in Gavotte I except B

C The chords to be played arpeggiando in Gavotte II   except D

Gigue Vivace ma non troppo allegro ♩. = 69

* On the string, heavy; middle of the bow

A The Bach-Gesellschaft edition gives ⟨musical example⟩ and ⟨musical example⟩

5 mins.

Printed by Caligraving Limited, Thetford, Norfolk, England

Selected
STRING MUSIC

SOLO VIOLIN

Berkeley	Two Pieces: Introduction and Allegro/Theme and Variations
Elias	Tzigane
Lorentzen	Quartz

VIOLIN AND PIANO

Berkeley	Concerto (*piano reduction*)
	Sonatina
	Elegy and Toccata
Musgrave	Colloquy
Nielsen	Sonatas 1 & 2
Norgaard	Fragment V

SOLO VIOLA

Matousek	Intimate Music (1968)
Pettersson	Fantasie

VIOLA AND PIANO

Berkeley	Sonata
Cooper	Variants II
Murrill	Four French Nursery Songs

SOLO CELLO

Burgon	Six Studies
Lorentzen	Granite
Lutoslawski	Sacher Variation
Matousek	Intimate Music (1981)
Nordheim	Clamavi
Norgaard	Solo Intimo

CELLO AND PIANO

Berkeley	Andantino
	Duo
Lutoslawski	Grave
Wood	Cello Concerto (*piano reduction*)

CHESTER MUSIC
14/15 Berners Street, London W1T 3LJ
Exclusive distributors: Music Sales Ltd., Newmarket Road
Bury St Edmunds, Suffolk, IP33 3YB